CAMBRIDGE

PENPALS *for* Handwriting

4

Workbook

Name

Class

1 Trace and write the joins.

    ph _____   *pl* _____   *bl* _____

2 Trace and write the words.

   the playful dolphin _____

3 Make and write noun phrases using one word from each of these sets.

	black	photograph
the	blue	phone
	purple	planet
a	sensible	blind
	plain	people

_____

_____

_____

_____

_____

4 Write your own noun phrase using words with *ph*, *pl* or *bl*.

_____

_____

Check:
- your joins from *b* and *p* are correct
- your noun phrases make sense.

Find two joins to tick and two to improve.
Rewrite them.

1 Trace and write the joins.

pu _____ pi _____ pe _____

bu _____ bi _____ be _____

2 Add the prefix to each of the endings. Write the words you make.

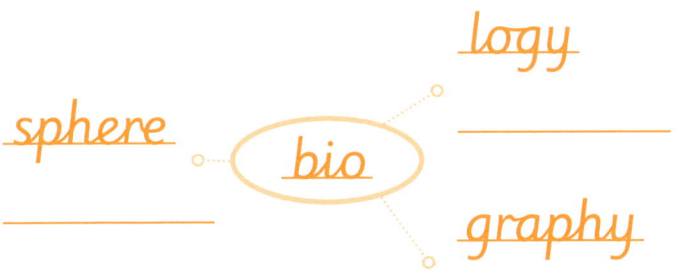

logy

ceps

sphere   bio   _____   nocular   bi   _____

_____   graphy   _____   cycle

_____   _____

3 Write two sentences using some of the words you made.

_____

_____

_____

_____

_____

Check:
- your joins from *p* and *b*, no ascender
- your spelling of your words with prefixes.

Find two examples to tick and two to improve. Rewrite them.

_____

_____

1 Trace and write the joins.

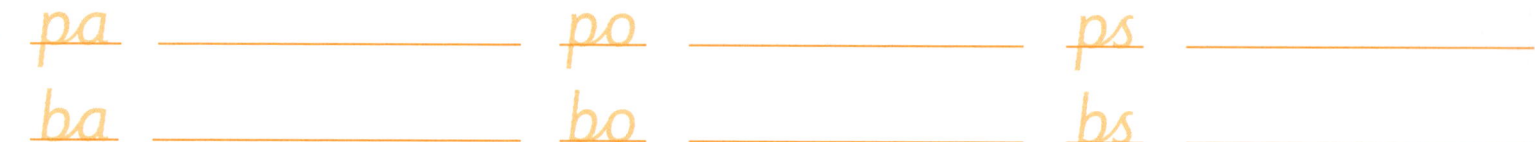

pa _____ po _____ ps _____

ba _____ bo _____ bs _____

2 Trace and write the words.

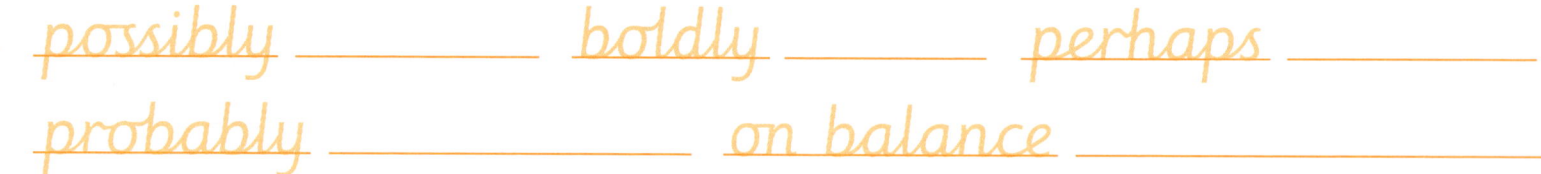

possibly _____ boldly _____ perhaps _____

probably _____ on balance _____

3 Complete the sentences using the adverbials above.

1. _____, I'll meet you later.

2. _____, we shall march up the hill.

3. _____, I will wait for you after all.

4. _____, I'd prefer to go on my own.

4 Write a sentence using the word *possibly.*

_____

_____

Check:
- your joins from *p* and *b* to anticlockwise letters
- your sentences make sense
- your spelling of the adverbials.

Find two words to tick and two to improve.
Rewrite them.

1 Trace and write the joins.

pp _____   *bb* _____

2 Add suffixes to the root words.

Root word	Adding suffix: *-ing*	Adding suffix: *-ed*	Adding suffix: *-er*
zip	_____	_____	_____
skip	_____	_____	_____
rob	_____	_____	_____
grab	_____	_____	_____
appoint	_____	_____	_____
gobble	_____	_____	_____

3 Write a sentence using a *pp* **word and a** *bb* **word.**

_____

_____

_____

Check:
- your ascenders and descenders are parallel
- your spelling of each word with its suffixes.

Find two words to tick and two to improve.
Rewrite them.

_____

1 Trace and write the break letters.

x _____　　　　z _____

2 Add the word beginnings to the word endings and write the words you make.

periment　　　　　　　　hale

_____　　_____

treme　　　ex　　　perience

_____　　_____

3 Write the words you made and sort them into the table. Note that some of the words can be both nouns and verbs.

Nouns	Verbs	Adjectives
experiment		

4 Write a word with z at the beginning, a word with z in the middle, a word which ends in z and a word with zz.

_____

_____

_____

_____

Check:

- your breaks to and from x and z
- your spelling of the words with prefix ex-.

Find two examples of break letters to tick and two to improve.
Rewrite them.

1 Trace and write the sentence.

"Why did the chicken cross the road?"

Rex

What do you get if you cross a kangaroo with a skyscraper?

A high jumper!

Zoe

2 Write the joke as direct speech.

Rex said

3 Write how many of each punctuation mark you used.

Check:
- your letter spacing in words
- your punctuation.

Find two examples of good spacing to tick and two to improve.
Rewrite them.

7

1 Trace and write the joins.

_in_ _____ _im_ _____ _il_ _____ _ir_ _____

2 Trace the words. Add a prefix from above. Write the new words you make.

Root word	With a prefix
active	_____
perfect	_____
mature	_____
responsible	_____
legal	_____

3 What happens to the meaning of the root word when you add the prefix?

_____

Check:
- your letter sizing
- your spelling of the words with prefixes.

Find two examples of equal letter sizing to tick and two to improve.
Rewrite them.

_____

_____

1 Trace and write the sentence.

Zane was reading his friends' books.

_____

2 Trace and write the sentences. Add the capital letters and punctuation.

1. the boys forgot the girls books

_____

2. the girls were excited about the babies toys

_____

3. the childrens favourite game was Z-Box

_____

3 Now add the apostrophes to show ownership of the books, toys and game.

Check:
- the size of your capitals compared to the size of your lower case letters
- your punctuation marks.

Find two words to tick and two to improve.
Rewrite them.

_____

_____

1 Finish the chart. Write quickly. Time yourself.

Personal pronouns	I	you	he	she	it	we	you	they
Personal pronouns	me					us		them
Possessive pronouns	mine			hers				

2 Write a sentence using all three types of pronoun.

_____

_____

Check:
- the chart. Swap with a partner. Is it correct?
- the smoothness of your handwriting.
Find two words to tick for fluency and two to improve.
Rewrite them.

_____

_____

1 Trace and write the word. Write another word with *ph* in it.

✏ _dolphin_ _____ ▢

2 Trace the words. Write another word with *bl* and one with *bi*.

✏ _blue_ _____ _bicycle_ _____ ▢▢

3 Trace the words. Write another word with *bb* and one with *pp*.

✏ _robber_ _____ _zipper_ _____ ▢▢

4 Join these words using the joins you know.

✏ _exercise_ _____ _amazing_ _____ ▢▢

5 Trace the words. Write another word with *im* and one with *il*.

✏ _imagine_ _____ _illegible_ _____ ▢▢

6 Rewrite and punctuate the speech in the sentence.

✏ _hello this is important_
please can you listen

Mark and score. ▢ /10

11

1 Trace and write the joins.

ll _____ dd _____ th _____ lk _____

bb _____ tt _____

2 Trace and write the words.

descended _____ disciplined _____

scientist _____ ascended _____

3 Choose a word from above to fill the gaps. Rewrite each sentence.

1. The _____ worked in a very _____ way.

_____

2. He _____ the laboratory stairs, looked
at the stars and then _____ again.

_____

_____

Check:
- your ascenders. Are they parallel?
- your spelling of the words.

**Find two words with parallel ascenders to tick
and two to improve.**
Rewrite them.

_____

_____

1 Trace and write the joins.

tion _____ *tion* _____

2 Make nouns by adding *-tion* **to each of these verbs.**

1. *observe* + *tion* = _____

2. *classify* + *tion* = _____

3. *imagine* + *tion* = _____

4. *prepare* + *tion* = _____

5. *inform* + *tion* = _____

3 Write the spelling rule for adding the suffix *-tion*.

Words ending in *t*: _____

Words ending in *e*: _____

Words ending in *d*: _____

Check:
- your break letters
- your ascenders are parallel
- the spelling of your *-tion* nouns.

Find two words with parallel ascenders to tick and two to improve.
Rewrite them.

_____

_____

1 Trace and write between the lines.

brake _____   break _____

meet _____   meat _____

peace _____   piece _____

great _____   grate _____

2 Write a homophone for each word. Write between the lines.

mane _____   meddle _____

scene _____   bawl _____

Check:
- the size of your letters
- the spelling of the homophones.

Find two words with good letter sizing to tick and two to improve.
Rewrite them.

_____

_____

1 Trace and write the joins.

ture _____ *ture* _____

2 Trace and write the words.

adventure _____ *captured* _____

signature _____ *picture* _____ *creature* _____

3 Rewrite each sentence. Check that the height, length and width of similar letters is equal.

It was an _____ storybook.

_____

The princess _____ the _____.

_____

She scribbled her _____ on the _____.

_____

Check:
- the proportion of your letters
- the spelling of the -*ture* words.

Find two words with good letter proportion to tick and two to improve.
Rewrite them.

_____

_____

1 Trace and copy the joins.

ssion _____ *ssion* _____

2 Make noun phrases using one word from each of these sets.

Determiner	Adjective	Noun
the	interesting	discussion
an	colourful	admission
a	surprising	expression
	curious	procession

_____
_____
_____
_____

3 Write your own noun phrase using a *-ssion* word. Watch your spacing.

_____

_____

Check:
- the spacing between the letters
- the spelling of the *-ssion* words
- the noun phrases make sense.

Find two words with good letter spacing to tick and two to improve.
Rewrite them.

1 Trace and write the sentence. Underline all of the words with an *ay* sound.

They are our neighbours from number eighty.

2 Choose the correct spelling for the *ay* sound. Rewrite each word.

w _____   ob _____

sl _____   tr _____

_____ teen

Will you use ai, ey, ay or eigh?

3 Write a sentence to include at least two of these spellings.

_____

_____

Check:
- the spacing between the words
- your spelling of the words with the *ay* sound.

Find two words with *ay* joins to tick and two to improve.
Rewrite them.

_____

_____

1 Trace the words carefully, then write them at speed.

roared _____ yelled _____

muttered _____ whispered _____

2 Choose a word from above to fill the gaps. Then add punctuation.

1. Get out of my way _____ the giant

2. I can help you to get down _____
   the rescuer

3. I'm not sure what to do are you _____
   _____ my partner

4. I'm too sleepy now _____ the child

3 Write how many of each punctuation mark you used.

"	"	?
!	.	,

Check:
- your punctuation
- your writing is easy to read even when you write at speed
- your punctuation marks.

Find two words to tick and two to improve.
Rewrite them.

1 Trace and write the words.

I was _____ he/she/it was _____

you were _____ we were _____

they were _____

2 Write the sentences below, correcting the mistakes. Write neatly and carefully.

1. We was excited about the cinema.

_____

2. I were going to get an ice-cream.

_____

3. They was excited too. _____
4. When we met up we was happy.

_____

Check:
- your grammar. Did you correct all
  the mistakes in the verb *to be*?
- the smoothness of your handwriting.

Find two examples of fluency to check and two to improve.
Rewrite them.

_____

_____

1 Trace and write the words.

mine _____ yours _____ hers _____ his _____

its _____ ours _____ yours _____ theirs _____

2 Write a pronoun from above in each of the gaps. Rewrite the sentences neatly at speed.

1. I like this bag; it's _____

_____

2. She has a new phone; it's _____.

_____

3. The dog is happy to see us; he's wagging _____ tail.

_____

4. They let us ride in their sports car; it's _____.

_____

3 Check your grammar. Write a sentence using a pronoun you did not use above.

_____

_____

_____

Check:
- the smoothness of your handwriting at speed
- your use of pronouns.

Find two words to tick and two to improve. Rewrite them.

_____

_____

1 Trace the word. Write another word with *sci* in it.

✎ *scientist* _____ ☐

2 Trace the word. Write another word ending in *-tion*.

✎ *invention* _____ ☐

3 Trace the sentence. Punctuate the speech in the sentence. Add your name.

✎ *I can punctuate speech correctly declared* ☐

_____ . ☐ ☐

4 Trace the sentence. Fill the gaps with the correct verb form of the verb *to be*.

✎ *We _____ learning about the* ☐

verb 'to be' and I _____ pleased. ☐

5 Trace the sentence. Add a possessive pronoun.

✎ *This is my handwriting check;* ☐

it's _____ .

Mark and score. | 8

1 Trace and write the joins.

ou _____ *ou* _____

2 Trace and copy the phrase. Keep x-height letters between the lines.

trouble in the countryside.

3 Trace and write the words.

country _____

loud _____

double _____

about _____

found _____

touch _____

4 Sort the words into words with *ou* that sound like:

young	proud

Check:
- the size of your letters is similar
- your spelling of the *ou* words.

Find two words to tick and two to improve.
Rewrite them.

_____

_____

1 Trace and write. Use the lines to help with checking your letter proportions.

The pyramids in Egypt.

3 Trace and write the words.

crystal

gym

python

mystery

beyond

rhyme

4 Sort the words into words with y that sound like:

myth	*sty* **or** *yak*

Check:
- the proportions of your letters
- your spelling of y words.

Find two words to tick and two to improve.
Rewrite them.

1 Trace and write the joins.

ous _____ *ous* _____

2 Trace and write the phrase. Check your letter and word spacing.

The enormous rhinoceros.

3 Make and write noun phrases using one word from each of these sets.

Determiner	Adjective	Noun	Prepositional phrase
a	serious	hippopotamus	in a muddy swamp
an	jealous	monster	in a towering rage
this	enormous	sister	under the magic mountain

1. _____

2. _____

_____

3. _____

Check:
- the spacing between letters and words
- your spelling of -*ous* words
- your noun phrases make sense.

Find two examples of good spacing and two to improve.

1 Trace and write the sentence.

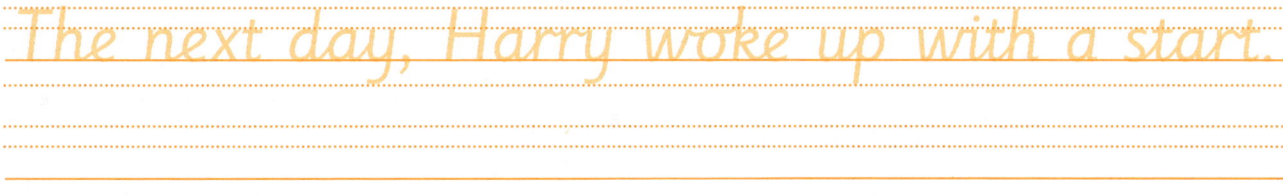

The next day, Harry woke up with a start.

2 Rewrite each sentence with a fronted adverbial. Check the size, proportion and spacing of your writing.

1. *Jarvia went to see Harry later that day.*

2. *Harry felt better the next morning.*

3. *They both went out after lunch.*

4. *They met friends in the park in the evening.*

Check:
- the size, proportion and spacing of your writing
- your use of fronted adverbials
- you added a comma after each fronted adverbial.

Find two examples of good size, proportion and spacing to tick and two to improve.
Rewrite them.

1 Trace and write the phrases.

I have done

he/she/it has done

you have done

we have done

they have done

you have done

2 Write the sentences, correcting the mistakes. Write neatly but at speed.

1. I done it really well.

2. We done it already.

3. They done it with us.

4. You done it better than I done it.

Check:
- the smoothness of your handwriting
- your corrections to the verb *to do*.

Find two examples of smooth writing to tick and two to improve.
Rewrite them.

1 Trace and write the words.

✏ *dis* _____ *dis* _____

2 Write each word twice without stopping. Tick the one that is most fluent.

✏ *misunderstanding* *disappointment*

_____ _____

_____ _____

3 Add *mis-* **or** *dis-* **to make new words.**

✏ _____ + *agree* = _____ _____ + *behave* = _____

_____ + *trust* = _____ _____ + *like* = _____

_____ + *lead* = _____ _____ + *appear* = _____

4 What happens when you add *mis-* **to** *spell***?**

✏ _____

Check:
- the smoothness of your handwriting at speed
- your spelling of words with *dis-* and *mis-* prefixes.

Find two examples of fluency to tick and two to improve.
Rewrite them.

✏ _____

_____

1 Write the pronouns.

I me mine _____   *you yours* _____
she her hers _____   *he him his* _____
we us ours _____
they them theirs _____

2 Choose the right pronoun from above to fill the gaps.

I {
Give it to _____.
It's _____!

I'll give it to _____.
It's _____!
} He

We {
Give it to _____.
It's _____!

I'll give it to _____.
It's _____!
} They

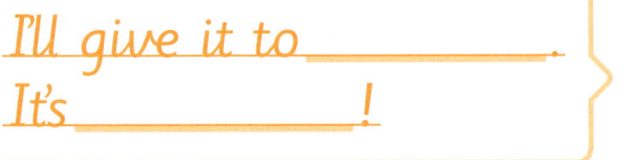

Check:
- your break letters are not joined
- your use of pronouns.

Find two examples of break letters to tick and two to improve.
Rewrite them.

_____

_____

1 Fill in the gaps to complete the alphabet.

_a_　_b_　＿＿　_d_　＿＿　＿＿　_g_　_h_　_i_　＿＿　＿＿　_l_　_m_

＿＿　＿＿　＿＿　_r_　＿＿　_t_　＿＿　_v_　＿＿　＿＿　＿＿

2 Now write the complete print alphabet with no exit flicks on your letters. So a not _a_, d not _d_.

a b c d ＿＿＿＿＿＿＿＿＿＿＿＿＿＿＿＿

＿＿＿＿＿＿＿＿＿＿＿＿＿＿＿＿＿＿＿＿＿＿＿＿

3 Write your name and address using print.

＿＿＿＿＿＿＿＿＿＿＿＿＿＿＿＿＿＿＿＿＿＿＿＿

＿＿＿＿＿＿＿＿＿＿＿＿＿＿＿＿＿＿＿＿＿＿＿＿

4 What do we use print letters for? Why?

＿＿＿＿＿＿＿＿＿＿＿＿＿＿＿＿＿＿＿＿＿＿＿＿

Check:
- your print alphabet letters.
  There should be no exit flicks
- the presentation of your print letters.

Find two examples of print letters to tick as well-formed letters and two to improve.
Rewrite them.

＿＿＿＿＿＿＿＿＿＿＿＿＿＿＿＿

＿＿＿＿＿＿＿＿＿＿＿＿＿＿＿＿

1 Finish each word. Write it in full. These are all joins you will find in your book.

1. ele___nt

2. ___anket

3. ___cycle

4. ___dal

5. pro___ly

6. ___ssibly

7. ro___er

8. zi___er

9. e___periment

10. ama___ed

11. ___portant

12. ___legal

13. l___ratory

14. imagina___

15. an enorm___ pyramid

16. adven___

17. discu___

18. We ___ (to be)

19. I me___

20. They ___ theirs

po　pe　im　x　abo　bab　them
ssion　were　mine　tion　ph
pp　bb　z　bl　bi　il　ture　ous

Remember to think about size, spacing, proportion, speed and fluency. Give yourself a score out of 5 for each.

1 Fill the gaps to complete the alphabet.

A _ C _ _ F _ _ _ _ J K _ _ _ _ _ _ _

_ _ O _ _ _ S T _ V _ X _ Z

2 Write these words in capitals.

danger _____   no entry _____

stay out _____   poison _____

no entry _____   one way _____

Check:
- your capitals.

Find two examples to tick as correctly-formed capital letters, and two to improve.
Rewrite them.

_____

_____

Certificate

for completing

PENPALS *for* *Handwriting* **4**

awarded to

NAME
_____

DATE
_____

SIGNED
_____

University Printing House, Cambridge CB2 8BS, United Kingdom

One Liberty Plaza, 20th Floor, New York, NY 10006, USA

477 Williamstown Road, Port Melbourne, VIC 3207, Australia

314–321, 3rd Floor, Plot 3, Splendor Forum, Jasola District Centre, New Delhi – 110025, India

103 Penang Road, #05-06/07, Visioncrest Commercial, Singapore 238467

Cambridge University Press is part of the University of Cambridge.

It furthers the University's mission by disseminating knowledge in the pursuit of education, learning and research at the highest international levels of excellence.

Information on this title: www.cambridge.org

© Cambridge University Press 2015

This publication is in copyright. Subject to statutory exception and to the provisions of relevant collective licensing agreements, no reproduction of any part may take place without the written permission of Cambridge University Press.

First published 2015

20 19 18 17 16 15 14

Printed in Poland by Opolgraf

A catalogue record for this publication is available from the British Library

ISBN 978-1-84565-385-9

Acknowledgements

© Cambridge University Press 2015
www.cambridge.org

Illustrations by Matthew Britton
Cover design and layout by me&him
Authors: Gill Budgell and Kate Ruttle

CAMBRIDGE
UNIVERSITY PRESS

www.cambridge.org